Whatever Shines

Whatever Shines

Prose Poems

Kathleen McGookey

THE
MARIE
ALEXANDER
POETRY
SERIES

White Pine Press
Buffalo, NY

All rights reserved. This work, or portions thereof, may not be reproduced in any form without permission.
First Edition
Library of Congress Card Number: 00-109780
ISBN: 1-893996-19-0
Edited by Robert Alexander
Series design and typesetting by Percolator
Printed and bound in the United States of America
The Marie Alexander Poetry Series, number 4

Excerpt from Marianne Moore, "Marriage," reprinted with the permission of Scribner, a Division of Simon & Schuster from *The Collected Poems of Marianne Moore*. Copyright 1935 by Marianne Moore; copyright renewed ©1963 by Marianne Moore and T. S. Eliot.

The publication of *Whatever Shines* has been made possible by support from Robert Alexander and with public funds from the New York State Council on the Arts, a State Agency.

White Pine Press
P.O. Box 236
Buffalo, NY 14201

www.whitepine.org

For Rhys VanDemark

Contents

III

I

"When I'm married, I expect to be thoroughly happy, making beds and washing dishes."

from my grandmother's journal, 1935.

Tale

I will not begin, Once there was a man who loved me. Anyhow, there were several, and only one persisted. We didn't speak of clothes, the self demanding all attention, all emotion: that was the bad part, and forward motion doesn't stop it, doesn't stop the wonderful moon. Still, I've nothing to say about him, his one tender gesture of laying his cheek against mine. The small house grows hot in the sun. I was like no one he'd ever known, he said. I knew better. By now, he has burned all my letters. He has buried the flicker that flew into his dining room window, and stunned, lived forty-eight hours. He laid it on a grassy hill, near ants. So it could have eaten. It could have lived. Though the weeks continue to turn and turn, he treats me as if I were small and young. I didn't ask him to drive by my window, to walk beneath. Though he later did in anger—small thrill. And then the moon washed us clean with its gossamer, attaching us lightly, lightly, to this world.

Lilies

She wants to lie down and drink the dark in,
the humid dark not far from a lake
where she watched a man she knew she couldn't love
swim back and forth among the lilies.

Two days later, his mouth's still all over her.
The lake makes it easier to breathe.
Too many times: a green park bench,
his lap, the fish restaurant, and him saying

Anything you want. The fish like silver coins.
Then six flights of stairs, no elevator,
an armload of lilies. The taxi home after the trains
stopped running. And even the cabbie wanted

to meet the following day. In the morning,
her second floor window, the teapot on the radiator,
her tapestry chair, the boys in short pants
under her window, on their way to school.

The boys pass her window every day
with their mothers, who wear skirts and red lips.
Her neighbor watches, leans out his window
and speaks to each of them, every day.

The street is the street of shoemakers.
A crystal chandelier in the dining room,
a portrait of great-grandmother. None of this
belongs to her, but she likes its quiet,

its museum quiet on a street of white lights, of shoemakers,
after a motorcycle ride, the country house, money in the air
and him close, offering a lily that opens
wet and huge.

Leda

Still alone, holding her breath and watching night fall
as in a Magritte painting: trees outlined in black
and a thumbnail moon carved in inky-blue sky.
Underwater, fish see this gold moon, each wave

with its own piece of sky, and six swans: two white, four grey.
All the plums fallen from her trees, the fire dead
and weather very nearly out of control. Her arms clean
and white and beginning to be strong. The six swans

not her obsession, yet they appeared daily. Her face grew pale:
she would not wish another swan into a man. To begin with, she said,
hands weren't worth waiting for. Then the problem of too much light;
afterwards, the lake began to freeze, hundreds of black

Canada geese honked on ice, and the swans circled
in smaller and smaller patterns. She let go
of their silhouettes, of the silhouette of desire,
of falling into the perfect temporary quiet of a mouth.

The swans like angels, like god, like bodies
on the sidewalk not quite covered by sheets. No comfort in wings:
even a tulip's slight curve is obscene in the wrong hands, even
roads curving, trees leaning in strong winds, even that

is wrong. Her hands smelled of garlic. Bonfires glowed
and smoke hung in the trees. She waited to be lifted
out of her body as she stood at the sink, dishes steaming.
Already she saw broken ice, the lake swallowing a man.

Vernal Equinox

The sweetness of the kiss cannot erase what came before, green words and potato's eyes sprouting, a clear plastic film over all the furniture. She almost goes with the wrong man, and we feel as dejected as the hero, losing her, but look!—she is not lost in the weather. Time and time and time, words perfectly still, the gray cat sleeping on the kitchen table. She thinks of the many men she knows, undressing, how their skin from this distance seems papery—she could rip it with a touch. But she stops. She wears the moon on a silver chain; the moon, the untouched moon, wouldn't sully itself if she were bad like that. She is alone, and birds fly breathless and stupid into her windows. At night, she hears the geese and the low lonely moan of the lake freezing, then breaking up. The birds sing for the fog to lift—it isn't quite spring, but soon these words will green and sprout. She is trying to be careful. She is used to being alone. She would rather be in fields anywhere, muddy, the pink and white farmhouse intact as a doll house with a light in the corner bedroom. Any empty sky, with clouds like fish scales pushed by the wind. Today she thought there was something magical about white geese waddling in the fenced-in yard, the charred house silent. The geese the opposite of loss, fat pillows, slow. Shut doors. Just attraction, the possibility that takes its shape as a man wringing his hands. And she goes wingless.

Swans

Swans in my front yard, my lake-yard again, dipping their heads to the bottom, to whatever they find under glittering water, under water shiny from sun. But what do swans have to do with loss? The end of summer? A third one now, a fourth, all over the yard and I'm better just looking at them. They seem reasonably happy, bright white in dazzling sun. Inside, the sun connects shadows to my pen, connects me to my sleepy dog. This can't be the last warm day of the year, four swans in a line, signalling. Soon I will have to write everything to remember it; I do not dream in detail. Light lifts itself from the ground. The sunrise stained the whole sky pink yesterday, so spectacular I didn't mind driving under it for so long. There aren't words left out here, just a few leaves in the trees, too many in the yard. Soon I will join the swans clean in the sun, in the lake's glistening waves. I know the lake has lost its warmth, I've seen it mornings giving up summer, giving up steam. I can't think of any substance I'd like transformed, straw into gold. But maybe that. Maybe myself slowly and secretly into a swan, for leaving.

Leaving Logansport

Esther walks along the tracks toward Bloomington, an idea in mind, mostly hope and being smiled upon, and can she pay it back? The snow hard and delicate and sparkly. Someone wrote his heart to her: we should be smoke, we should be sky. She could hear the neighbor disciplining his son in the back garage. She smelled of vanilla. The idea that one was wanted: Matt, then Arthur, then Ross, only carefully alluded to in her photo album. Here the tennis pro gazes so intently down her shoulder there's no mistaking the emotion. I love to see her laugh and hold the banjo. How then does she refuse herself and the hard slick stars shining above, the moon in its hazy cloak? The departure, having been conceived, is a way of carrying herself through the days. She had promised her mother. But could she pay it all back? A uniform made of yards and yards of white cloth, the sky stained pink like a gift in the east, fog spills from snow-covered fields to the road. Once an idea takes hold, the heart isn't satisfied. The heart that owns her is a swan's heart, happily lording its white pieces over her in the sun, but the frozen world won't yield. It is hard to be related to royalty in one's blood. But she is, and she is visited on a regular basis by the ghost of a white dog, the white dog that owns the crying neighbor boy in the shed. The sun bursts inside her. I can't see her face for the hat.

Meteor

What it looked like I can imagine: lightning
over sumac, a long tail and loud thud in the dark
and the neighbors came out of their root cellars
to see the sky open in a frenzy of wings.
Not one leaf on the large oak was torn.
No animals behaved strangely, no signs of
inclement weather, this night a meteor
fell to the family farm, 1920, Union City.
We've always expected what's predictable, silence
from the stars and my grandmother Esther,
who thought the swift light a vision,
herself changed—there, in her summer nightgown
watching her father calm the neighbors
as the moths flew to her, to the inside light—
and she was the vision, as I've always wanted to be.

A day can split any number of ways,
the night too . . . and thereafter wildflowers
sprouted near the meteor, itself quite solid, thigh-high.
The neighbors kept coming through the violet-scented night
and into the following day. A priest was called.
The children were kept in from school. Did she feel chosen,
my grandmother who hadn't driven a car, who admired
the neighbor boy's goats and new corn? Being near such power
was reason enough: neighbors looked for her hidden wings.

Class Picture, My Grandmother As Teacher, 1922

———

There's no knowing what she knows, no small, sad smile,
just a steady gaze, her hands carefully placed
on the arms of the wicker chair. Absolutely still
for minutes, as the photographer clicked and muttered

and fussed. She gazes out of the chair.
She sees the first snow falling, dizzy patterns,
and the big eighth grade boys—she's afraid of them—running past.
This day of expectation, a carriage ride, a white rabbit muff,

and a certain dignity lost, a word, once said,
that cannot be called back. Each time smoke rises
from the black stove, she claps the lid down,
then returns to the front of the classroom, something like fear

in the back of her throat. Her hair smoothed back
with a big navy bow. Some children
she loves less than herself, and the boys
would be better off in the fields, far from her, better caught

in moonlight in hay, not half-tamed
in class, bodies spilling off their chairs.
Her hair is smoke, the smoke that rose
as her father's barn burned, and eight men on horseback

formed a half circle around the blaze and simply watched.
Slow music and tall buildings rise in her mind.
She'd rather the photographer were gone, the children too,
and the books expectant in the empty room.

———

English 105

I wear a suit the first day because I can't say what the suit says. When I ask my students to list the places they've slept, one asks, What exactly do you mean by that? *Taste of onion in someone else's mouth, sweat drips like tears, the busty lady at the beach changes under her towel.* I mean only and exactly that, I reply, though it is too late, the innuendo has already escaped into the room. It is a cold spring, so the classroom is pleasantly cool. And quiet—after the beginning Japanese class next door leaves off its low monotone of "Good morning, how are you?" The trouble is that we are all too aware of our own bodies. The trouble is I have lost my double, who wanders off to the shade and picks up a watering can. But the lush green lawn is not for us; you'd see that, if only you'd read the signs. Can you read? Can you swim? Well, someone's got to jump in the lake to rescue the lost boy who's fallen out of the canoe. He planned this accident to escape his father, and look at his hard luck! Here we come to put him back into his father's arms again.

Gladys and Her Kindergarten

Pentwater, Michigan, 1915

No one said you mustn't do this: so many little Indians with bows drawn. So many little Indians, all in one sharp line. Feathers blurred, fingers blurred, and one is turning his head. An unhappy animal hides itself in the woods nearby and cries and cries, among the ferns and dogs, the children's breath, the birds. My great aunt Gladys in the middle, sitting slightly behind. No one's smiling; here are their best, serious faces, and no one's feathers have come undone. Gladys smiles and strikes a pose, brief and gracious. Everything can be a lesson, a way to live, though there are consequences: the single note of a bird, two notes really, and the answering bark of a dog. Some smile afterwards, price of the photo worth this alone. This one with long blonde hair—if a child can be like a daisy, this, surely, this is the one. It isn't so bad to imitate what one loves, to transform oneself, occasionally, with flowers and wings. They can amuse themselves for hours, they have wings! No sense repeating: feathers, feathers. And winged children, somehow, drift safely in planes overhead. One can wait with a fixed expression though it doesn't feel like waiting, though friends will whisper, then later write: she never married anyone. White teacup, clean kitchen, cooking for one. Disguise the daily routine: walk to school, if possible, in new shoes. Understand the bounds of money and weather, restrictions to live within. Empty snakeskin to show the children, delicate and crackly pocket of skin.

Wedding

A hawk landed on asphalt
I drove by

The sun washed down a white house
I remember feeling done with envy

Then glitter and pink tulips
Grandfather still in his thin house

Children danced in evening clothes
Giggles rising quick

No rising sun
No white piano

No one had a knife
But the bride's father had a microphone

Under our plates we had lottery tickets
No one said if you win, give them half

Simple Arithmetic

I am still imagining the men lined up, the ones I imagine who want me. I'll tell you everything I know: there was a boy, a girl, and a boat. And palm trees, but the mosquitos on the island chased them back to the boat. There was a boy, a girl, and a dog: I still can't get the story straight—magic fruit? straw into gold?—and night's black velvet has arrived. I am glad for my life and the high clear voices of four-year-olds in the Allegan Public Library. I am not the girl in the story—I am the girl whose mouth is mainly shut but who imagines it open. But where are the other boy and girl? Holding hands and walking into the library while a baby falls out of a pile of money with astonishing grace. She's afraid to go beyond the normal bounds of conversation, the simple arithmetic of the heart. An electric blue butterfly darts in front of the car, just beyond reach and the camera's focus. The clocks tick, their greedy faces shine. The money will always fall out of our hands. We will always be slightly out of place, standing behind ourselves, not getting anywhere—no island, no boat, and no one to save us.

Logansport River Story

The wrong girl was saved; the wrong girl drowned,
though brother rode the horse into the river
for her, for her sorrowful hair. The picnic basket
was overturned on shore, the red pickled eggs forgotten.
The other family began to hate the Heddes, stole
jewelry and potatoes from the live girl's home.
Didn't they deserve something small?
The Heddes prayed the ghost away, prayed away
the stilled swan in their hearts. But they had
the saved girl, Hedwig, without wings by the river,
thinking it easier to die than follow red roads back,
mother's emerald ring lost, her own wedding
a dream of bad satin dyed black, black
because it covered stains, black because
how could she love a man more than the river?
Altars and doves and a dumb hope carved
on the lost ring, a dumb hope in her chest rising
when Hedwig looked at the trees in the yard, the cut wheat
stacked in the field and she in a white dress and hat,
happy—the river that loved her running behind,
offering its sorrow to the same sky.

Another Drowning, Miner Lake

———

A woman drowned last night in our lake, she was drowning but we didn't know: we saw flashing lights, a police car drove by our house. Drowning: the helicopter landed and all the cars backed out of the driveway. We heard on the police scanner it was a woman or a girl. Though her chance was slim, the sun set as usual, gorgeous and temporary despite the rain, a small sweet promise to our skin from the world. Promise of green, a gray dawn, a day that stretches long and without kisses or appointments. As much as we'd like to think we're elevated, we're not. We thought she was a little girl but it turned out she was older. We hadn't known her and still we swam, knew this about her, swam to the diving raft and someone's yard light shone white over us. No one can blame the lake; concentrate instead on saving yourself, myself, the self I have covered with wings, because today the lake is simple and gray and going through the motions, calm—flat as a plate, polite as any gilded mirror.

Lake Anniversary

That is the joke—thinking something had been promised, as though by keeping our mouths shut we would get the candy or the largest piece of pie. The silk of longing is never worth what we are paid: delicious motion, delicious, unstoppable rage. I am new at marriage and winter though I've had my share of unspeakable loss. It depends on the day, on the slant of light. A quick wash of color, a blink; I am fearful of birds and the quick flipping fish hauled from a frozen lake. Couldn't we have done better if we'd put our minds to it? It's hard to fathom where the hours go, yet they vanish into the slinking shy sunrise, into the dark that doesn't protect anything: not possums, not raccoons, not even the cows, composed and mooing in their enclosures. The silver coins give me a way of placing myself in your hands, but something is always lacking no matter how I save and spin. This wicked heart isn't itself today, can't forgive, can only add and subtract. Why, then, hasn't anyone said what she means, why can't we explain what to do, where to go, how to begin? Can we rise and take flight? Someone has tossed strings of glittering beads into the pine trees, out of reach. I'd like a letter, explaining what could have gone wrong, and then what actually did.

Line From a Journal

———

"When I'm married, I expect to be thoroughly
happy, making beds and washing dishes."

from my grandmother's journal, 1935.

I don't believe you meant that, but maybe you are happy,
maybe, that newly married moment in 1935 as you sit writing
while your husband visits the men in his Benton Harbor office.
Maybe then, so different from when you came home
to dishes after school (were you always doing dishes?),
the water cold and greasy, the fire dying, the black saucepan
you could barely lift.

You sit writing, half in and half out of the light,
making sense of your latest good fortune. Are you always a little afraid
it is a dream? Not only a dream of being warm, finally,
but of having enough: money, coal, new furniture and books,
no rain. A cool moon shines on your last night
as nurse's supervisor. Will you miss your job? Your name?
But still, this is no dream, you thought the ceremony real,
then the tall grass bows down as you drive to Traverse City.
Your silver ring etched with orange blossoms. Your brown suit
with lace at the throat. Fallen gold leaves so thick you can't see
the ground. Stray dogs run behind the car, happy in their wild eyes.
Rain, and then your car arrives on the terrible scene: you place
your husband's clean handkerchief over the man's face,
apply pressure to the chest. It is terrible, the only crash
you've seen right after. You bite your own cheek raw.

At home, your dogs in their cages sniff and groan. You watch the jays
and the lake and the flames. You bend over your cookbook, determined
to poach an egg and set a table correctly. You write,
and watch the moths fly to the light.

One Night I Will Invent the Night

One night I will invent the night,
full of cats with green eyes and golden dogs, night
of longest nights, where schoolboys walk past purple houses
and look over their shoulders at me.

I don't accuse them of anything. Before night fell,
in Pennsylvania, three Mennonite girls stood under a waterfall,
fully clothed. So it's summer. And no one thought sex,
but of water's

form and weight and how girls and water fit together
neatly. Someone else draws in details:
an old blue man plays guitar, skinny dogs wrestle in town.
Still, we are frightened by the horses and don't know

about the pilgrimage, all the cowboy finery.
And one horse lies down. Is it dead?
A motorcycle does wheelies for several hundred feet.
I'd be lonely in places I've loved, how I was different:

no one looks sadly off bridges, leaves fall, the water accepts.
The night I want: not completely dark, moonlight
on the dog, on the bed; no dogs bleed on the floor;
dragonflies whir, believing every person could save them.

Holds last week's moon: low, red, and large,
so large I could have driven into it. Holds all the minnows
that jump in sync at the slightest sound: minor waterfall.
No loss, no pale heartbreak of day.

A Small, Other Way of Living

The baby turns himself in the high chair and screams, I rush to free him, I rush and don't know what to do. A gray feather is stuck to my bumper with dew. Turn the day, turn the problem to milk, a sheet, a blank page. The light isn't blue. It is a clear blessing I may take advantage of, all explanations for sun and water used up.

Seen from the corner of the eye, the back of the room: a young woman or girl at the water's edge, writing. Though I imagined the scene, I left parts out. The house is only rented and no one can own the lake. I hesitate to mention passion, though the boats and ropes and cloudless sky have fueled themselves from it.

After so many times, what I say sounds worn and tired. Easier to say, I clean and fish and watch the sunlight travel across the yard. My mother lived this way. Easier to begin with ripe apples and sun, heavy bags of apples, half-eaten apples scattered below the trees. The smell of burning leaves. Really, no one is interested but me, so asking questions will not help. The reflection of sun on water moves across the ceiling. Why is it admirable to show restraint? Voices carry across water so I hear a little of what I'd rather not.

Reticence

——

I've no business knowing your beloved's pattern of love cries, or what your friend's child died of. Or just how deeply your sister was cut and how the edges of her wound resembled a sliced-open, vigorous plant. Please, close the door. How does your child like showing up for all the world? They might all be lies, you say. They might be literature. The world is sad without them. Maybe. But there is more to what I'm saying than complaint. Why can't you just change the names or the situation? Such as, a yellow bird flew into my window yesterday, then hopped away, dazed, and sat on the deck a long time. How did air turn to glass with no warning? Bird against glass upsets me. I'd rather have the pure and distilled emotion, if possible, like when I asked my family if they'd ever seen anyone left at the altar. That's what I mean. My father had, but couldn't make himself understood. And see, I'm not going to say why. The little tea shop is closed; I've pulled the green-striped awning in. Why not be satisfied with the raspberry jam and tarts, the door banging softly in the wind, and even though he couldn't speak, how my father noticed the flock of small white birds dipping over the lake at sunset before the rest of us, how his face followed the flock that moved as a single body, climbing, flashing blue, then turning away?

Raleigh's Journal:
Miscarriage, June 1936

———

At Big Star Lake, my grandparents gathered lilacs
heavy with the perfume the wind brings.
And what it takes away—
the expected child's room cold, door shut.

Last night a raccoon ate the sparrow's eggs,
shinnied the greased pole, emptied the nest.
And today, only a slow, absolute rain,
tree frogs and their happy chatter,

their backs gleaming like jewels, not diamond,
but soft-edged and green, then gone.
More than anything, my grandparents wanted to move forward:
they drove through water up to the runningboard,

they sold the pup with the most white
in its face. When the mist rose,
they could see across the lake.
Fish glittered like coins, like silver platters.

Five swans in a line, paddling,
and my grandmother heard piano music rise from under the water.
The picnic basket lay in the back seat, under a white cloth.
Almost every nurse, herself included,

had been amazed she didn't die. Even her sister
came from Logansport for one last talk
while my grandfather planted gladioluses at the funeral home
and wrote about the pups and eggs to be sold,

and the rambling rose in the backyard;
he said it would be lovely, lovely by the end of July.

II

"Jim gave me a diamond ring for Christmas and I'm wearing it now. I gave him shaving lotion—not a very equal exchange."

from a letter my mother Mary wrote to her parents on December 25, 1960.

Wet Velvet

———

Luckily there is a back door so the bride doesn't get drenched in her new best dress. The photographer borrows a red umbrella for the last shot: the couple dashes to the car, but she drops her bag in a puddle. Damp pause. Extra sheen, extra glitter of dress under water. No use saying *should*. No use saying *make yourself useful*. Closed mouth, wet velvet. No gaping. But ready for the illusion to crack and split around the inadequate reason. Something about resilience? A child hiding in the bushes must be found. Another has skinned her knee. The toddler grabs the flamingo by the neck—to uproot? No, to kiss. Giggle, sloppy peck. His small mouth a small hole. He walks unsteadily into the garden reception, not outdoors where rain pours and shows no sign of stopping, but indoors, which is carefully constructed to look like something else. It seems sometimes she prefers the cold and the wet and cannot be called back. She peeks for the car at two a.m. in the dull, undrinkable light, still thirsty. After a certain age, girls get questioned closely. Sometimes by family, often by strangers. The answer flares, an angry bloom: poppy, mum, bearded iris? A dozen red roses in her bouquet, alone.

Three Weddings in October

How do you give up your names so easily,
like old coats, like bright shells?
Gone like Saturdays near Lake Michigan, heat
and jumping dogs, collapsing tents and pines.
Lost just this year: Wilkins, Winslow, Burris,
while the deejay spins and calls, "Ladies and gents,
for their very first dance, Mr. and Mrs. . . ."
And when the light hits your shiny cheeks,
when you gather your uncontrollable dress,
why should I blame you? The hall table
is piled with gifts; all we can do is raise
rented champagne flutes and wish you well.
But your satin and daisy bouquet stains
me; it bounces near me, it lands near my name.

A Fine Evening

It was a fine evening, we'd say later, a fine evening followed by an even finer morning: a misty sunrise stained the sky pinker by degrees. Light fell on the blue thistle and did not change its nature. A mole followed his star-shaped nose underground, in his private inky sky. Time has never stopped just for me. When the fog lifted, we saw the dew like jewels all over the lawn. Then multiple veils, multiple jewels, and grandmother's ribbon of thought was privately unlaced. We had planned a romp in the park, but she kept saying, "You're on a long vacation; you're certainly far from home," when really *she* was far from home. Her daughter kept trying to straighten things out. Well, why not try to improve things, even a little? She said she had nothing to wear to the picnic, even after we said her suitcase was in the car. In the park, high winds had blown the sunflowers' pale petals away: the bare centers were stark on the stalks, and the stalks had fallen over. The crows in the trees would not stop their rustling, their raucous whispers. When grandmother sat on the blanket, she said, "Do not help me, I am full of tears." We had argued about what kind of candy she'd like. I'd let my morning glories die because I didn't think the weather, such good weather, would last into October.

Labor Day

———

Raleigh and Esther close the cottage because of the war.
If we can't all be happy, we will be a country
large in its sorrow. An exaggerated sense of responsibility.
This is what they wished for: how the sun

makes leaving bearable, how the amber light breaks their hearts
because it won't last. The lake stretches before them;
their daughter wakes to the martins' rising song. The key turns,
the heart turns inside its own wrong weather.

What makes return impossible? A shortage of gas,
a shortage of oil. But they have a little light:
Esther rides her blue bicycle around the lake,
and their daughter smiles behind her stringer of eight trout,

behind a certain slant of light, the lake's calm eye.
They will remember the light, how they bathe in it,
always the light and the lake. Never mind the soul's weight in water,
what water does to the soul. A slow and sure exit,

a great calm space. Loving only the martins,
Raleigh, behind the shed, begins
the last day drowning sparrows, English sparrows,
quickly and with so much care.

Purple Martins, 1970

Even if pictures tell the truth,
whose hand cradles that month-old purple martin,
like the new moon cradles the old? Hers?
I can see the wrinkles. One pert black eye,
a seed, dull light, and feathers sharpened to points.
And after, did my blue-eyed grandfather drop the bird
to its nest? Did their hands brush?
My grandparents kissed and laughed across the table
in Christmas movies, her hair dark, his shirt pressed. Once she tumbled
into the lake on a shoot for Audubon—
he rescued the camera first; the expense!

This picture is taken to show the band;
a thin metal ring encircles its leg
but this baby bird doesn't scare.
I've held them myself, hands cupped full of feathers and skin
I can almost see through, skin like that on my grandfather's hands.
Their hearts against my palms, my eyelashes black
against my cheeks, I look down, down at my hands.
The dark calms them, my grandfather said,
so we'd lift them to his leather satchel,
then squeeze the metal bands with pliers
while their parents scolded and divebombed our heads.

People mailed him the bands they found
from birds killed on highways or dropped
who knows why. He sorted them into glass jars
while I spun on his office chair,

then held down one electric typewriter key
in a long metallic wail and it sounded like he was counting
his pocket change, like nails spilled
on a cement floor, or like smooth white stones
dropped into a lake, one by one, everything lost.

Migration

(Raleigh R. Stotz, 1893–1981)

He becomes light in his bones and refuses
to discuss money. Instinct tells him, keep moving,
soon you'll be home. His hair is white.
He once wore a white tuxedo
with a red rose on the lapel,
but that was long before this winnowing.

It isn't intentional.
Others will not remember it like this,
like following a candle, one light
across a darkened field. When the car doesn't run,
he's not surprised: machines cannot be trusted.
Though he is becoming hollow, the weight of coins
keeps him on earth. He must pay all debts.
He has hidden his watch and his wallet.
He has spent his whole life gathering wings.
When the feathered cloud rises and swells,
he'll be ready.

View

The unhappy bird in my chest won't stop flapping its wings. The way I see it is the way I see it. The bird's underfeathers are blue, just below plain brown, so I can't call it sparrow. How is the view from there? *My heart was in my mother* is another way to say *I felt sick*. Or anxious or worried, because my mother says my father has lost some of his good sense. Once he woke himself up coughing; now he coughs instead of sleeps. Why should the body act like that? He melted his new glasses when he burned the brush. The neighbor tells me my father is a sharp man, meaning smart. But I watched my father turn on the kerosene heater in July when we cleaned the garage, and then he couldn't shut it off. Wishing cannot change anything. I chased the dog into the empty lot, among the neat piles of grass clippings, as soon as I smelled smoke. In the refrigerator, the tea changed into something bitter and dark. According to the checklist, the one I just happened to find, I'd already made almost all the critical errors, all the *don'ts*. But not quite everything. I'd saved everything, all my errands, for a day in town.

September, Miner Lake

The lakes hold their submerged anchors and cool flat fish, the delicate white flowers which have not yet lost their gloss. I feel sorry for the taxi driver who's spilled all my dimes out the window. A flash of lightning and then wanting to paint spangles all over my body. Not wanting to go and then being gone, nearly in the same breath. Today if you told me sunlight would heal me, sunlight and crisp wind, I might believe you. We are all in need of a black velvet cloak and an orchestra playing waltzes while we walk home in the rain. A woman I know pours salt and glittery stones in a bowl, then leaves them outside her window at night. The simple shine of an apple on the table, waiting to be painted. If anything, I'd like a love letter and too much light in my eyes. But I know better. Dogs follow me and lie at my feet, breathing their golden breath. My father is driving to Chicago today, to see another doctor. This obvious world tires us and that's all it's good for. The white lawn chairs are lined up and waiting for us.

At the Piano, June

Music drawn across sky:
beautiful arc, nose to forehead, nose

to lips and chin. White, white skin.
The line believes itself: look, a life story.

Hands clasped,
a voice that will not leave or sing,

strong, square chin.
Little light, ice spilled like glass

in the road. Black notes rise,
black butterflies, heavy in the sweet air.

Christmas, 1960

My mother lived a year in a cold country
to perfect her French accent, to learn to express her thoughts
on politics while my father, one country east of her,
spent his days decoding the military secrets of the Czechs.
I'm reading old letters, letters from my mother to her parents,
the year she lived in France. Christmas morning, thirty years ago,
and I'm not there, but somewhere
in Germany there are Jim and Mary, not married,
not even engaged, and a Norwegian girl, a friend
who drove from Tours to Tirschenreuth with my mother.
Look at those three, making small talk, decorating the tree.
I'll see Greg, my mother writes, I'll just tell him
I'm about to be engaged.
What other secrets has my mother kept folded for years?
She couldn't have expected the ring,
despite what she said in that letter, not knowing
what she wanted, as even her friends told her.
Every night she talked with Madame as they made dinner;
I see the warm kitchen, pots boiling,
my mother on a three-legged stool, trying to shape the language
into sentences she could live with.
How long can you put words that aren't your own
into your mouth? She draws a picture of her diamond.
She knew enough to want to say yes, after
Sunday visits to chateaus with the other man,
one with 300 chimneys, peacocks, and they let you walk the roof.
A chimney for every day. So how many days,
how many days, shadows on silk
on the inside walls. My mother lived in a cold country.
My father knew enough to ask,
while the cold wind blew through the stones of the chateaus.

He put the ring in a box of chocolates and worried
she wouldn't want any. But that same night,
somebody made ornaments from the foil wrappers that still
smelled sweet. And somebody made white yarn dolls for the tree.

Near Drowning,
Ihla Comprida, Brazil

———

Evening comes so slowly it is mere discovery; small white flowers blossom in my spine. The market opens—so many times with just a little money, mouth open in front of shiny dead fish. A small boy wants to carry the flowers I might buy. So far I've bought nothing and I plan to leave empty, I plan to leave slim so I can easily slip into what's expected of me, another skin. It is a matter of saying no to everyone. A matter of taking my body into the ocean, beyond where the waves start, but something in this story has been left out. We thought we were gone to larger currents, almost heartbroken, salt water in our mouths while crabs scuttled sideways up and down the sand. Yards out, taken further by each wave. Those watching us from shore were alarmed. Wouldn't it be stupid to die this way, with bright pink passion flowers growing near the gate? Later, salt air came through the car window— I could hear the waves as we drove across kilometers of hard wet sand. We didn't die. We weren't even sure, looking back, what the danger was, but birds circle my balcony, and if anything, I feel I've finally done something right, something as simple as sitting quietly, alone at the end of the day.

———

Instrument Factory, Brazil

It's simple enough to give away the coins in your heart, when dust settles over a pool filled with mineral water and the dogs, those sleek guards, raise their inky noses to a silver saxophone moon. Beyond Saõ Paulo, down a dirt road, men make French horns, flutes, and cymbals with the delicate precision of angels. Blue-suited, they sit at tables: one tests a saxophone, another welds the key of a flute. And each has tools on the table, a candle, a blue welding flame. Stacks and stacks of half-finished instruments crowd the factory aisles: bells of horns, all sizes, rows of French horns hung on a green metal rack, pyramids of tambourines and drums. I love to watch their mouths emerge, but I have closed my own against the men with their suit coats hung over their shoulders. Our guide runs his finger across my cheek, then down the elegant neck of a flute. And the slim scraps of brass, shaved off, curl like hair when they sweep the floors. Here, they use plastic for clarinets; even the good wood, when they can get it, rots in the sun. Behind us, a young boy plays scales in a testing room while vats for nickel and brass plating steam behind windows. And the workers walk with horns slung over their shoulders, the almost obscene curves shining in their closed hands.

Overnight Ferry, Yugoslavia: Ljubljana to Split

The man on the ship said it would be nice to hold my hand. The un-shaven man in the next seat with teenaged kids back home. Yes, that sloppy man said it would be nice, my hand. He said he was famous and had money. He offered me some. I thought, why not throw my saucepan and tortoiseshell eyeglasses into the sea and proclaim myself a duchess? Couldn't it happen? But it wasn't a ship, it was an overnight ferry. The tea was oily and the duchess could not bring herself to take a sip. We passed a loaf and a knife back and forth until I put them away. Marmalade sun shone through a jar on the ship's windowsill; I left the ship to walk the boulevard under the palms. The cars were nothing to be afraid of, but the long afternoon was, so many hours to fill with a map, walking and looking for a room. Even in the museum I heard the ocean and the palms rustling in the sunlight outside the white walls. I'd exchanged my backpack for a small silver key. On the museum grounds, the bushes trimmed into animal shapes almost hid the mar-ble statues rising out of them. The garden seemed wild, overflowing with growth, but the wildness was carefully calculated and the plants did not overgrow the sidewalks. When my nose began to bleed, I had only my two clean hands to stop it.

Tulip

———

Water poured from the mouths of golden bulls, and music played from up in the trees. Really, I couldn't say when my kisses got closer to his mouth, or when he began crossing busy streets to get to me. He had a certain unapproachable quality—do we seek in others what we lack? For a moment, I was unable to speak, even near water. The heart is in the middle, badly drawn and soggy. It's difficult to predict when I'll feel this generous again. It began with a picnic near a fountain with a gendarme. The rest of the schoolgirls were jealous, until they heard she simply couldn't shake him, how he'd drive by her window at night and leave things by her door. No one wants that relentless, sickly attention, a wilted tulip, brown at the edges. We'd rather find our own signs in the sky, in the water that's always running somewhere in the back of our minds. No use beginning with the police report, a young foreigner chased back to her apartment, signs of a struggle and still she can say she overcame him. It wasn't me he was after, she'll say, partially in comfort. It was the idea of something unusual, something elegant in its bones. We want, and we want. Mainly they watch how we walk and pause.

Second Date

———

The movie felt like porn: a couple had sex, then lay by the campfire, naked, to show her boyfriend when he returned. Betrayal didn't bother him, so they all had sex in the shower. Did my date want me to get ideas? Afterwards, we walked in a park, lingered on a green metal bench. A man photographed the angel rising behind me and the granite sparkled in the flash.

My date asked if I could store my contact lenses in kitchen spoons, with a bit of water and salt. His friends liked his room so well, he said, they begged to borrow the key. We were ten flights up, near the pigeons, under the eaves, far, far above the cars on the Boulevard St. Michel. Noise didn't rise that high. Two windows with balconies for morning coffee. What could be more beautiful than pigeons in the moist and rosy dawn?

Mont St. Michel

The family cottage was closed, François said, and unlocked a small dark sitting room with furniture draped in sheets. The ceiling somehow too low. So we would find a hotel, no? Sneaky. He'd said, Let's spend the weekend in the country. At his parents' house. Properly. A hotel wasn't the plan. I was sure I'd understood.

The first room had a big double bed; François buried his head in my shoulder. I was shorter so he had to lean. He said he wanted twin beds. I let him pay. I was a stranger in his land. Call it greed. Call it wanting to be swept off my feet. But he sat and watched me read. He borrowed my soap. I played dumb. At breakfast he buttered my bread, in love with gesture. That afternoon, we climbed to the top of a lighthouse. The dark green fields were full of fluffy sheep, as he'd promised. Then we ate bouillabaise, made of clams in purple shells, the shells yawning open, clams emerging like tongues. I licked one clean, to keep.

Another Question of Travel

—

We think we own the lake by walking its circumference, pointing to our own rented lot—*there*. A blue heron flies over the interstate, but why travel? The landscape of the heart stays the same. We are not singing this simplest of songs, the hurts were small, really; the lake could swallow them all. It is still the time of night before dark comes but I know it is coming. I am thinking of how uprooted trees smoldered in large piles in the fields all last week in the rain, three tight lines of smoke rising. The trees seemed too large for any force to have done that kind of damage—slow orange fires despite the rain, the next day soot-blackened roots. Today I'm interested in reduction: the smallest size, the quickest way. Summer's ripe desire fades from the days, color removes itself from skin, leaves, flowers. Still, I have a little light left. When I saw the armored guards loading money into their truck, it was a way to reduce the most complicated problem to dollar signs. There's no owl in the dark and the mourning doves sit complacently on the sidewalk until the dog quivers and can't stand the challenge. I used to equate being rich with having enough time, though now I know better. A dog is barking itself into my morning. Maybe we can catch ourselves before anything is lost, but already my words are rising into the day, already half the town has driven through the pearl-gray dawn.

—

Hands and Cameras

———

The birds didn't mind being cradled, being hand-held, days after birth, then weeks, and the parents didn't reject them though they smelled of hands and cameras. But what was Gladys Snauble, my great aunt, doing in Tokyo anyway? Holding birds? No, she's standing in front of a temple, a group shot. She never married anyone. In Tokyo, a deer ate from the women's outstretched hands. Not Gladys, but a postcard she sent. The situation is difficult but not impossible to explain. The deer could venture closer because that was its nature. And the same for the woman in the red blouse, it's her nature simply to be approachable, though she and the deer are essentially alone in the world, the only other structure a birdhouse in the shape of the tin man's head. I am being honest; remember, I like you. As for marriage, Gladys will be the first to explain: girls hang off the caboose, pretending to be brakemen. Girls smile and smile and silently add up their weight in journals, neat rows of numbers, their burden on the world.

III

She says, "This butterfly,
this waterfly, this nomad
that has 'proposed
to settle on my hand for life'—
What can one do with it?"

Marianne Moore,
from "Marriage"

Song

You say it is easy to confess, then walk away, but I've heard enough. I wish your lovely white lady would get it over with and descend, descend again to you like a flurry of pigeons or doves, or land like snow on the lawn. Something must be green because new love smells like grass. I'll watch from my seat at the curb; I've got my sandwich and sunglasses, and after the bicycles pass, like silly geese speeding after each other, of course she'll be standing on the other side of the road, petting the chained elk. So you'd have me believe. But you're not quick enough—you rise from your chaise lounge, fold your newspaper, or stumble, or tie your shoelace, or someone asks you for the time, and when you turn back to her, she's gone. Couldn't wait or didn't want to. Maybe she wanted to lift herself out of herself. You were already thinking, you've confessed, about how her hair would look on the pillow, how you'd balance on one hand and look down at her. But she's changed her life, why can't you? Because some of the trees have died, leaving behind their red leaves which rattle after the bicycles. The elk is lonely, too, think of how lonely, day after day, getting his picture taken with whoever wants him. But she, of lovely, indescribable color, she's something else. You swear she was right there.

No Elegant Catastrophe of the Heart

It can't get worse but it does. She leaves. She never loved you. What is real and what has been imagined? This is not an elegant catastrophe, it is messy. Was she ever there? You divide the dishes; she takes the tv. The garden's overrun with zucchini and tangled vines, so it's no surprise that she—the princess—has turned back into a toad and no matter how you run, she hops through the mud to the cabbages. Then a skunk sprays the dog and you must spend hours bathing it in tomato sauce. Why not gather the rotten tomatoes and take aim? Still, you have some dignity left: no one fell from the roller coaster though you held your hands in the air. Meanwhile, I search for the perfect word to console you, though even the lake today is inconsolable, mist drifts to the road and still the sun's a bright orb behind it all, fuzzy and shining. Where is the hope in this? What word will protect you, change it back? The essential damage remains—your heart, your broken eardrum. Nothing fits: not my clothes, not my body in the house; even the pets suspect I am counterfeit and eye me suspiciously. That's what is left: eyeing and sizing up . . . while the rain erodes the garden beyond explanation.

Picture of Radiance

My own failings are far too evident: all day long I have wanted sleep and a letter, something brand-new and packaged. I must tell someone else's story. How about the bride who was the picture of radiance in her off-the-shoulder dress in Indianapolis two days ago? I, with my small heart, noticed the hors d'oeuvres. Wished for more food, less talk. Only the family got champagne. Was that rude? To be so obvious about pouring it? There I go again. Money. Love of it. I don't love it, but I worry. Try this: early evening, Indianapolis, and I watched at the hotel window for the long white limousine to drive by. We didn't want to be too early to the reception. I didn't, anyhow, and when we arrived, we accidentally took someone else's seats. How were we supposed to know? This is still her story, but look! we had to pay to dance with her or the groom. It was unexpected, the deejay's ploy, and we didn't do it. We said, instead, how cheap. Then someone from our table got cake for everyone but me. So I went to get some: sickly sweet butterscotch with nuts.

June Afternoon

Still, the other choice, always the other, appears more attractive. Shall we go arm in arm into the fountain, to cool our feet? The earth will take us all back. The proud children hold the stringer of fish, the string of birds, the weight of their bodies approaching the earth. It's harder than one might imagine, a long string of written words, eventually trailing to yes. The setting is perfect and would you believe that music often rises in the afternoon as though on a current of air? Here in the attic there are empty trunks and stacks of books and heat enough to fill your chest and cloud your vision with anxiety. People look, and the looking matters. With this much time, I could write my life story and people would clamor for its completion, someone would knock gently then take my hand. I have finally figured out all the machines here, which come with the briefest instructions. As for the story of my life, it's still forming, though how interesting is it? She stood by the window, the frame painted blue. Or, she seems to desire something, though she can't put a finger on it. Or, she walked in the woods, through Queen Anne's lace that grew over her head, like nothing she had seen before. Here is a fountain with two stone cats intently watching. I've been told to walk as if I'm the happiest person on earth, to place each foot into an open lotus blossom. If I were truly that happy, the earth couldn't hold me down.

Stranger Than Fiction

—

A sinkhole swallowed a house, a gorgeous and decadent house. Nothing could be done! The house disappeared underground in a matter of hours, the velvet upholstery unruffled, the tassels and chandeliers trembling. In that house, they must have amused themselves for hours. Certainly they had time. This disturbance came in the night, rather near dawn. Night faded as we lived in its tattered grace, its evening clothes, as the house moved in regular motion under the earth. Even the sparrows quieted themselves, as a larger sound grew behind them: a hunger of years, the sound a heart might make in the midst of a mistake. Someone at the sewer department in the city will surely have to pay. If the earth suffers such terrible hunger, what could begin to satisfy it? Not one house, not books and trees and telephone poles. Though everyone must feel it, a constant ache. Or maybe I'm the only one. I could walk around all day suspicious, checking over my shoulder, then under my feet, for light shining up through the earth.

Complaint, Personal

My elbow hasn't sprouted mouths and neither has my palm. I'll say this once: not everyone burns. Not everyone is *on fire*. If everyone shattered half as often as you say you do, I'd be stuck driving my pick-up through the shards to work. I'm a poor schmuck. I manage somehow, somehow, to hold myself together. Please stop that seventeen-year-old girl from running circles in the field: you put her up to it with your talk of burning. So it's your voice in her mouth. She's really thinking *daisy, moonlight, silver violin.*

I value the moon. I value forgetting urgency, the dash to the phone that's yanked out of the wall. The moon will always come back. But you fool yourself: the fire isn't real and I am sick of it even from this distance, across the page. Can't you say anything else? Don't flatter yourself and imagine I am talking only to you. Everyone in the world can hear—if they'd only put down their teacups to listen.

Elegy for Stan Hudley

(1914–1996)

What I remember most is not universal truth but it is mine: Stan in a t-shirt mowing the lawn, his broad bald head shining. I always thought he made sense though my mother said she'd seen it before: he'd gloss over weeks and months, unsettled to find memory gone or changed with no putting his finger on why. He called his granddaughter's boyfriend, then husband, Lover Boy. But in the end it didn't matter. He was a grandfather and mine was gone; he was next door. I thought, how nice. How nice to see him though he later sold the place and talked earnestly of the deal. Whose details, including price, changed according to the day.

At the picnic, he apologized again and again. He said, "If only I had known." On the way, we had taken a corner too fast and three bean salad spilled on the back seat. Even if I dedicated myself to cleanliness, things would get stranger, not better. A woman of mops says in an anguished voice, *my clean floor!* The state of cleanliness is not constant and the floor belongs to everyone. Like the road and the act of crossing it to get to his granddaughter's high school graduation. And the confusion and sirens that followed. At the picnic, he called me my grandmother's name. There is more mud here than is reasonable for spring, and no goat-footed man walked the trails near the beach. But deer have left tracks and eaten so many tulips that now no one pities their hunger.

Imaginary Letter About the Weather

Soon, you will put your message in a boat and send
the boat downstream, downstream to me. Can a letter

contain light, or the clink and splash of dishes?
Look what's lost: gifts for the heart's own weather:

tiny tea sets in the shape of watermelons, silk fruit
with the patina of bloom.

But now the weather's changing: slow constant rain
all afternoon. Or high winds. Or hail.

Now you have something to write me about,
instead of goldfinches alight on asparagus in the field,

the doe which bends to its fawn. The red sun
sets like a jewel, bright in its clothes. Soon, soon,

call the doves. The sun a great egg pining in the sky.
Not for me, but someone like me. Trick of the eye

or weather: how far away am I, am I walking in a field,
just one person, not two? I walked to my red mailbox twice today,

and the storm remained the same: a guess, an expanse of wing,
a leaf blown across water. Clear like the ring of a bell.

When will the fish surface and swim behind me? Soon, soon,
call the doves, dusky in their trees.

The Moon in My Grandmother's Watch

My grandmother looks away from the camera. She says
she's unattractive, an old woman, an empty glass.
Her first patient left silver spoons and sent picture
postcards from Switzerland. Touch them and the phone rings:
tonight, there's an eclipse over the lake. My brother
tells me, Go to the window and watch.

Picture this scene. Picture
my grandmother, young, on a train. Men watch
as she leaves her seat, then forgets her rings
in the bathroom. She travels with her brother.
The dining car fills with the music of trembling glasses.
He doesn't want her to marry. This is what he says.

Hours after they met, my grandfather bought a ring.
This is true. A diamond, not the flawed glass
star I've held on my finger. My brother
says the constellation is shifting: he can picture
her nurse's uniform, her profile, but he can't say
he misses her. He watches

the sky even as he talks. Each mirror, each plate glass
window in his house reflects the world pictured
in her Time-Life encyclopedias: we loved the stars, the glossy rings
of Saturn. But the moon in my grandmother's watch
has stopped. She holds her wrist to her ear, she says
something to the camera. This is the one my brother

wants. He can say this much: he says
her tidy black jewel box burst that afternoon. Her gold watch
was new. She sifted cool pearls from bracelets. We drank glasses

of ice tea and left rings
on the mahogany table. She wanted a picture.
She wanted all of us in it: me, my mother and brother.

Tonight, the stars make diamonds in the waves. As I watch,
only a slight ring
of the fish moon becomes visible. If what we love turns to glass,
how do we keep it safe? The stars say
nothing; they bury their mysteries in light. No picture
rises out of itself. But my brother

is happy. My brother has his telescope; he'll watch
for hours though the glass, then wake, his eyes ringed
in black: the gilded stars, he says, only outline her picture.

One Possible Story

No light, just a sense of satisfaction, something sweet on the tongue. I don't know every story, only the story of lake and field, high and clear and away, sense enough to stay out of the woods. Here I am singing in one hour wrung from a silent clock, a timeless day, a day so empty it leaves me breathless. But all that luxury adds up and some-one must pay for the single swan on the lake, though the lake itself is gone. There will be light and time enough to hope, to still my soul and the dog in the yard. A single swan in water the color of sky, gray, and the light gone, but the sky still streaked with roses. It isn't dark and the dog's in the yard. Our lake is solid gray but not yet frozen, holding all my dogs and fears and letters home. It is too quiet here for such fierce love, but begin the story again, how they met in a museum and then he cooked her dinner. How did she have courage? Or were they stand-ing in a crowd watching street musicians, a juggler, and he offered to take her picture? Were they both far from home? I'd rather not know, rather continue the afternoon as though I owed thanks, inside my own happiness. No one has written that story about me, but someone keeps an envelope of my hair in his sock drawer, as I keep the lake's strength to myself, the doves and dogs and rain.

Block Party

Then voices. Then silence. Then the sky rumbled. Shivery light forked on the horizon. Don't blink. I ran to set out my tin can. Then rain poured into the basement and washed all the cardboard boxes away. But now the sky is lit with clouds and patches of blue. No one's screaming. The doves sit on telephone wires, dreaming dove-dreams where all the hunters fall and rip their jeans and scramble home to change. The metal pails dream of brimming, overfilling—and then the moment when it spills, water's brief life. Still, no one's screaming, such a messy word; it's awkward, like *flailing*, or *failing*, when something's wrong no matter how carefully the evening was planned. Most events go on in the rain, though they'll have to rent a white tent and the doves that are released will bump into the ceiling. What were they dreaming of? Telephone wires, that's right, and the thousand thousand conversations rushing through their claws. Thick voices. Long pauses. Was that the baby screaming? No, just someone crying over sheets dried on the line, and the children who rode through them—look how the walls disappeared!—on tricycles. It wasn't planned or schemed; the sheets presented themselves, a sunny day, an expanse of green. Someone sold the dream of sun and kids on bikes, a block party where we all eat berries and cream. But they set up the tables in my grandparents' new garage, on account of the rain. Inside the rain's hush, the doves rustled their wings and practiced their soft calls. Calling here, here, here. Calling me.

The Wrong Kind of Grace

Called away to look through the window—the heron poised, then walking through the yard—I say yes, this view of the heart, this visitor, is better. The wind is either pleased with me or not, and will blow until notice is taken. It shakes the porch windows, the waves come toward me. The story has already begun, though everyone's still waiting for the surprise twist. For free tickets to the fair, though that involves money and a whole flock of crows rising up from the road, the dog rolling gleefully in manure. Now the swans return the same day a man drowns: coincidence.

I had one white dress and gave it away. The problem remains: I'm still in love with the idea of motion. Though I've made a decision, I can't live up to it: there's water in almost every direction. Look, here is the road I drive home. I live on a peninsula, or I should say we do. This is not a riddle: the important part must come later, news from a man wearing a hat. Or just a man. Or just some news, some forward motion, smiling faces, a red sailboat on the water, moving, and not too fast. Or walk in a certain, selected direction: past the raspberry bushes, past the gravel pit where deer gather.

Poem for My Mother,

who said, I'll bet you can put *that* in a poem. Here are the guests throwing water balloons at my wedding and later, Clarence shooting his rifle at water snakes. Two houses down, Jack shoots raccoons from his living room couch; think what you will but it's quite a nice neighborhood. Here I am riding in the backseat with my mother's old ladies; Margaret Lubbers fell asleep on me and I thought she might have died. Most of all, here I am alone at a party for high school friends, one so fat now she might be mistaken for pregnant though she owns a lovely firelit lakeside home. Because they didn't hear the doorbell, I thought I might not have to go in. Still, I sit by the hearth and clap for the engaged couple and think, a house like this can't make you thin. Which is the truth. Which does little to make me feel better; I am ashamed of my heart and still haven't mentioned Diet Coke in crystal goblets and chatter and bone-white hope and panic when the person who spoke to me most went across the room to wash dishes. Would they ever cut the cake? I can be rude on the phone but not face to face. How about the weather, how about the fishing up north? Look. The way I see it, if we get enough rain, we could just drift away.

Honeymoon

⸻

The animals are sick with love. A white dog
walks the beach like a shadow. A blue heron perches
on the dock, its long neck one deep loop.
Someone was eating roses and reading

love letters while the sea turtles ate out of our hands.
I want the heron to stay. It could have good news.
I could be what it wants. You have to put your face
in the water and breathe, the woman says,

breathe, and the bubbles grow until they surface,
where I float with the jellyfish, where I'll catch them.
I'm sorry I feel this way. There's a spider
on the towel I've just used to dry my hair.

The string quartet followed them into the garden,
the sun shining and all the boats on the lake
gathered out front, and happily,
no one fell into the cake. Acres of sunflowers

bent their bright heads to the bride.
One must surface slowly for all kinds of reasons.
Your lungs could explode. Look,
I can't tell you what's wrong,

it's very loud and the air rattles my mask
like too much rain. I am crying with a stranger.
She asks, "Are you doing it for him?"
I am sick on the beach on a white towel, I am sick

and doing it for him, the animals are sick,
and the parrotfish swim close because I want them.
Why are the beaches deserted and the restaurants empty,
why can no one serve us what we want,

a simple sweet piece of key lime pie?
Animals are stamped on silver coins.
It's not too late to ask the blue heron to stay,
to drop what we can't carry, but listen,

I'm not going to beg. There are no love letters on the reef.
When it rains, we run to the covered part of the boat:
everything begins here, including bad weather. Here money
is no object, and we pay and pay.

Irises Rising

After agreeing to marry him, Anabelle became an expert on fine and delicate lace. Some have heard this story before. You must embellish a little: they live in his magnificent basement while his house is constructed. It is a question of money. She stays alone so much just to keep an idea in mind: the lace comforted in the midst of change, though back home they wondered what she could have meant, sending such a picture of herself, such a glare? Now all the boys want themselves in black and white next to her. The cut glads are in baskets on the step. They keep a list of who would like flowers, then deliver them regularly. She is happy, though birds fly into her windows, and grows larger in the laws of universal control. Meaning grown men don't stick their hands into fountains. Meaning truth is difficult and swans are best seen from a distance. She loves light and wants it to come naturally from the mouths of people she loves. Though it may not rain, wet leaves and mud may not comfort her, spring brings a certain degree of satisfaction that's been lacking. She can't say what she's dreamed of all month—not the president or angry dogs, or fires and irises rising up from the ground. How many wild animals has she seen and from what distance? Fifteen deer and one yearling move in fluid lines from field to field. At close range. Such grace.

Bird in the Pines

It is easier to be compassionate when one has time: I took strawberries to the old woman who lives down the road. I helped another one to her car. A butterfly lay on the dirt road and I picked it up by its wing. Already in writing it, the event has changed: say I saw right away the butterfly's body was crushed, say its wing smudged my thumb. Say it rained all day and all day yesterday and ruined the strawberries in the field, which leaves me at the old lady's door empty-handed. I am done with compassion; I wish someone would tell me to stop, to get down on the floor with the dog, where I could admire light from the window coming through glass vases. So it is a small thing, change of self, change of light. Already what I meant to say is further away than when I began: the question is reduced to whether the dog barked when the real estate agent unrolled her yellow tape measure. Or whether the lilting bird in the pines kept calling its two-step call into the day, into me.

First Month, New House

———

Still, we keep beginning. We believe we can start fresh, forget arguments over water in the basement or whose cat scratched our screens. We agree a limit exists though it's hard to pinpoint. Of course its location changes: the lake lies further away and noise from cars and trucks breaks through any calm, any silence I find. We compare new and old: no doves and swans, just a rooster crowing without regard to the day—started without his bidding—which he cannot call back. A cricket calls from the front hall closet. There is a field here but no other sense of possibility. It is never evening, just night and day and night. The radio tower's red lights blink in the front yard long enough I realize it's no signal, it's not even a sign. Maybe this is the sign: the moon stays in the sky into the morning; the moon must love the world, I can't imagine loving anything so much.

Addendum

But I *can* imagine loving something that much; I wanted to say so from the beginning, even though I knew some would call me sentimental. The waves froze, it appeared, just in the act of rearing up—though it must be more complicated, no sudden snap, just a gradual drop in temperature. I like to walk in the park and get water in my boots. He says, surely we could have planned better, surely we could have planned more. The words on yellow scraps can't live up to themselves.

So he smirks at me from across the page. He says, look at the finches in their summer color. He says, take a book out on the lawn. I say, can't you let me have one moment to myself? Talk of vegetable perfection makes me think of giant tomatoes and corn dwarfing the house. By slippery blisses, we mean something fleeting. An exquisite mouth can explain itself.

Last Night, An Owl

called into the dark, over and over.
The mourning doves only cooed, stupid enough to stay
in the road. It could end here, my half-constructed grief
for the girl I might have been, dressed smartly,
speaking another language in a cafe.
Desire of my own making hangs around me: I share an ice cream,
lick by lick, in front of the subway station; I go off
with strangers near the quiet fountains slimy with moss.
Someone is breathing outside my window.
It's as if I'd never left, or wanted to,
this strange cycle: a wedding, a body other than mine,
a warm house, a dog.

We could see the owl in its nest, growing. But the leaves came
and we forgot it there, flying and calling at night, calling itself
into my sleep where someone was giving me a gift.
But here are two seagulls bothering the loon,
here is the dog with a dead rabbit in her mouth. Here are my mother
and grandmother still in their bodies with the child reaching
for the mirror.

It may sound crazy but last week I interviewed a woman
and halfway through, thought I *was* her, watching myself talk.
I am waiting for a day where the light is in the sky before I am,
and pours itself into me. I can't look.
I am not singing. I am not confusing the mist over the lake
with the light I am looking for, the absolute word.
Finally, enough fireflies and sleep. A small ache.

Whatever Shines

―――

At first, you don't turn the antique coin, don't feel the chip in the crystal, the dented armor, you just coo in admiration. You simply close your hand around whatever shines—a gift to keep but never look at, like the luxury of traveling somewhere together in a car. You open your mouth and I kiss it; you are holding something under your tongue. This weekend you said the word *lover* over and over again until it was lost. You wonder what it's like to be the first and last face I'll see in a day, but you left the garden a long time ago. Not any garden, but the garden where we've never been together, the garden where a father twirls his daughter in a circle in the lake. She wears a red bathing suit and throws handfuls of water in the air just to see the shapes it will take. Her front teeth are gone. A yellow tiger lily opens while a woman on the shore smiles sweetly and waves to the camera. What if nothing remained but the motion of her hand to her chin or her cheek? She removes her white hat and combs her hair. It shines like the gold domes of universities. You know her. She waves to the man and the child out in the water, and to you. The water is rising up to join her, but you don't see it. You are writing our names in the sand.

Snow

I want only to be home, and hurry, stupidly, twenty miles an hour
too fast and still twenty under the speed limit; my car skids,
then spins and stops. The man in the next car says, if you don't mind,
my neighbor can pull you out, offering this meekly, *if you don't mind.*
He's good like a boy in grade school, and I'm lucky to be lifted
near this light. I can't find the hazard lights on my dash.
I could have killed someone, I could have been killed,
and before I think this melodrama through, his friend lies down on the ice
to hook up the towstrap and I'm grateful and closer to home.
One summer night, mayflies gathered near streetlights in downtown Allegan
thick as snow. Then Village Market clerks brought out their cans of Raid
and when we drove home, the mayflies
popped under our wheels. We might have missed it.

Angels in ice, in stained glass, spread their invisible wings
and stop children who tumble out of cars and trees. Even my inconvenience
is only that, not pain, no money lost, no one dead.
My car went off the road. Someone helped me. The high wires buzzed
with energy, laden with ice. My life is too little to speak of.
That's true, this poem wasted on it, while the hyacinth bulbs over the sink
just begin to bloom. The house is so cold some days
I can see my breath inside. My imperfect windows leave the sun
in my eyes and children in Sarajevo run home from school
through cemeteries. The dead never come into the house,
a girl says, but bullets have. She's not afraid of the morgue. Her friend
just says he runs zigzag, and fast, so fast they can't catch him.
But one morning snipers shoot children as they play in new snow.
There is calculated evil, and calculated risk. A perfect white blanket
of snow. And no sign of another day, yet one comes,
then another, with terrifying regularity.

Acknowledgements

———

Acknowledgement is made to the following periodicals, where some of the poems appeared, sometimes in different versions:

Birmingham Poetry Review: "Raleigh's Journal: Miscarriage, June 1936"

Black Warrior Review: "Lilies"

Cimarron Review: "Snow"

Epoch: "Purple Martins, 1970," "Near Drowning, Ihla Comprida, Brazil," "Irises Rising," "Leaving Logansport" "Lake Anniversary," "No Elegant Catastrophe of the Heart"

Faultline: "Tulip," "Reticence"

Field: "Last Night, An Owl," "Honeymoon"

Gulf Coast: "First Month, New House," "Bird in the Pines"

Hanging Loose: "Whatever Shines," "Wet Velvet"

Hawaii Pacific Review: "Meteor"

Indiana Review: "Logansport River Story" (as "Hedde Family Tree: Logansport River Story"), "One Night I Will Invent the Night"

The Interlochen Review: "View"

The Journal: "Migration"

The Laurel Review: "Elegy for Stan Hudley"

Luna: "The Wrong Kind of Grace"

Madison Review: "At the Piano, June"

The Missouri Review: "Leda," "Simple Arithmetic," "Class Picture, My Grandmother As Teacher, 1922"

New Poems from the Third Coast: "Block Party," "Line from a Journal," "Poem for My Mother"

Notre Dame Review: "Another Drowning, Miner Lake"

The Party Train: An Anthology of North American Prose Poetry: "Instrument Factory, Brazil"

Phoebe: "Hands and Cameras," "Gladys and Her Kindergarten"

Press: "Three Weddings in October"

The Prose Poem: "September, Miner Lake"

———

The Prose Poem: An International Journal: "One Possible Story" (as "Untitled")
Puerto del Sol: "Christmas, 1960"
Salt Hill: "Tale"
Sundog: The Southeast Review: "Another Question of Travel" (as "Untitled")
Verse: "English 105"
West Branch: "Imaginary Letter About the Weather"
The Worcester Review: "The Moon in My Grandmother's Watch"

I'd like to thank Sharon Bryan, Cullen Bailey Burns, Nancy Eimers, Dirk Jellema (in memoriam), Yvonne Murphy, Jack Ridl, and Bill Olsen for their help and encouragement. The Ragdale Foundation awarded me a residency during which I wrote some of these poems, and the Arts Fund of Kalamazoo County and the Irving S. Gilmore Foundation awarded me grants, all of which I gratefully acknowledge.

Kathleen McGookey earned her MFA and PhD from Western Michigan University. She has taught at Hope College, Interlochen Arts Academy, and Western Michigan University. Born in Grand Rapids, Michigan, she has lived in Michigan all her life, except for one year when she lived in Paris. Her work appears in the anthologies *The Party Train: A Collection of North American Prose Poetry* (New Rivers Press, 1995), *The Best of The Prose Poem: An International Journal* (White Pine Press, 2000), and *New Poems from the Third Coast: Contemporary Michigan Poetry* (Wayne State, 2000). Her poems have also appeared in literary magazines including *Boston Review, Epoch, Field, The Laurel Review, The Prose Poem: An International Journal,* and *Quarterly West.*

THE MARIE ALEXANDER POETRY SERIES

Volume 4
Whatever Shines
Kathleen McGookey

Volume 3
Northern Latitudes
Lawrence Millman

Volume 2
Your Sun, Manny
Marie Harris

Volume 1
Traffic
Jack Anderson

—Forthcoming—

Moments Without Names:
New & Selected Prose Poems
Morton Marcus
Spring 2002